BY SWORD DIVIDED

✐ Corfe Castle in the Civil War ✐

*Thirteenth-century seal of
Walter, Clerk of Corfe Castle*

ANDREW NORMAN

HALSGROVE

First published in Great Britain in 2003

Copyright © 2003 Andrew Norman

Front cover picture: *Corfe Castle in the Beauteous Isle of Purbeck*, 1940
by Isabel Florrie Saul, oil on canvas, 55x61cm
© Russell-Cotes Art Gallery and Museum, Bournemouth, UK
The Bridgeman Art Library

British Library Cataloguing-in-Publication Data
A CIP record for this title is available from the British Library

ISBN 1 84114 228 X

HALSGROVE

Halsgrove House
Lower Moor Way
Tiverton, Devon EX16 6SS
Tel: 01884 243242
Fax: 01884 243325
email: sales@halsgrove.com
website: www.halsgrove.com

Printed and bound by
MPG Books Ltd, Bodmin

CONTENTS

ABOUT THE AUTHOR

Andrew Norman was born in Newbury in 1943.
He was educated at Thornhill High School, Gwelo, Southern
Rhodesia, now Zimbabwe, and St Edmund Hall, Oxford, where
he read animal physiology. In December 1970 he graduated in
medicine from the Radcliffe Infirmary and went into general
practice in Poole. In 1983 he sustained a back injury
which forced him to give up his medical career.
He is now a writer, and is the author of:
T E Lawrence: Unravelling the Enigma,
Tyneham – The Lost Village of Dorset,
HMS Hood – Pride of the Royal Navy.

PREFACE

Corfe Castle stands on a hill of moderate size in what was traditionally a royal hunting sanctuary known as the Isle of Purbeck. On either side, much higher ranges of hills give added protection to the proud fortress. Beyond the castle's walls lies the town of Corfe Castle, with its church and cottages. Here, in the first half of the seventeenth century, with her family and men and maidservants, lived Lady Mary Bankes, wife of Sir John Bankes, Chief Justice of the Common Pleas and a Privy Councillor.

Throughout the realm a bloody war was raging between those loyal to King Charles I, and those who supported the Parliament with which he was in conflict. Mary Bankes's allegiance to the Crown was unquestioning and she kept Corfe Castle out of the hands of the Parliamentarians for three long years.

At the start of the struggle she was faced with an agonising choice. She could either surrender, and thereby place the lives of her children and household staff at the mercy of those she called 'rebels', or she could attempt to enlist the support of her wider family, namely her friends and the people of the town, and resist the attackers. It was a decision she had to make alone, for her husband was attending the king at York. Mary Bankes did not hesitate. She was of noble birth, originally a Norman and proud of her ancestry. She would not surrender.

ACKNOWLEDGEMENTS

The author is most grateful to the National Trust for permission to reproduce images of artefacts from Kingston Lacy and also to quote from Lady Bankes's account book and papers of Sir John Bankes. He also wishes to thank the Institute of Art, London; Picture Library, Windsor Castle; Wilton House; English Heritage; and the Corfe Castle Town Trust for kindly giving permission to use their pictures, which are individually credited, to illustrate the text.

Many thanks, too, for their help, to the staff at Dorset County Museum, Wareham Museum and Dorset County Record Office. Also to the Reverend Stuart-Sykes of St Stephen's Church, Kingston Lacy, the rector and churchwardens of Wimborne Minster and Mr H W Drax.

And a big personal thank-you to Jean Norman, Mary Hurst, Jane Francis and Catherine Hubbuck for their advice and encouragement.

1

MAY DAY 1643: THE FIRST ATTACK

Mary Bankes's problems began on 1 May 1643. This first day of summer was traditionally celebrated throughout the country with a holiday for all, the crowning of the May Queen, and dancing round a birchwood maypole decorated with flowers and ribbons. The revels, which harked back to the Roman Floralia and Druidic feasts in honour of the god, Bel, varied from place to place.

In Dorset's Isle of Purbeck the day was marked by the coursing of a stag, for which permission was always formally granted by the lord of Corfe Castle, which stood at the very heart of the so-called 'island', which in fact is not really an island at all. This annual stag hunt was a great occasion involving the mayor and barons of Corfe, and the nobility and gentry from all parts of the island.

Hunters and hounds moved off in pursuit of their stag, and Mary Bankes remained with all but one of her children – the eldest, Alice, had married and was living at Oxford – in the castle set on a steep hillside of such symmetrical proportions as to appear man-made rather than a natural feature of the land-scape. It occupied a strategic gap in a line of hills which ran east–west for a distance of ten miles. 'Corfe', the name of both the castle and the town, derives from the Anglo-Saxon *corf geat –* *ceorfan* meaning to cut, and *geat*

Mary Bankes.
An enamel miniature by Henry Bone.
Photo: The National Trust

Corfe Castle as it was in the sixteenth century. The drawbridge, the twin towers of the outer gatehouse and the massive oak gates are in the right foreground.

meaning a gate – hence 'cut-gate', or a gap or cutting in the hills which in this case rose on either side to a height of more than 600 feet.

The previous year she and her husband had come to the conclusion that a period of civil unrest was likely to result from the continual differences between the king and Parliament, and they had, therefore, thought it prudent for her to move with the children to the country rather than for the whole family to remain in London.

It appeared to have been a wise decision. Throughout the winter and well into the spring all had been quiet in the Dorset countryside – but the net was closing in. Parliamentary forces under the command of Sir Walter Erle had recently taken possession of Dorchester, Lyme, Melcome, Weymouth, Wareham and Poole, leaving only Corfe Castle loyal to the king.

Heavy head colds prevented seventeen-year-old John and twelve-year-old Ralph from joining the May Day stag hunt. The other boys – Jerome, eight, Edward, six, and Charles, four – were too young to do so and all the girls stayed at home. Mary, twenty, was the eldest, then came Elizabeth, sixteen, Joan, fourteen, followed by Jane, Bridget, Ann and finally Arabella, who was only a year old. Unbeknown to them several troops of Parliamentary horsemen, their drab uniforms in stark contrast to the colourful attire of the Cavaliers who fought on the side of the king, were setting out to capture the castle, which their commanders wanted to add to their other garrisons and so secure the Dorset stretch of the Channel coast to the rebel cause.

They were planning to ambush the stag hunters and then to take the undefended castle. However, matters did not go the rebels' way. News of their intentions had leaked out, the hunt had dispersed and Lady Bankes received warning of a possible attack.

She immediately ordered the gates to be shut against all comers. The drawbridge spanning the deep ditch dug in the reign of King John was raised, the huge wooden gates closed and drawbars fixed in place to make them doubly secure. The massive portcullis, an oaken grille faced with a layer of beaten iron which acted as a fire-deterrent and worked by a system of counterbalanced weights, was lowered.

Above the portcullis in the two-storey twin-towered outer gatehouse, built during the reign of King Edward I

An arrow-loop window in one of the inner gatehouses.
Photo: The National Trust

(1272–85), there was a slot through which intruders could be bombarded with hot embers and stones. Each tower contained a guardroom with its own fireplace and arrow-loop windows in its walls, which enabled the castle's defenders to identify friend or foe without risk to themselves.

A contemporary account of what happened next is described in the *Mercurius Rusticus*, a newspaper which supported the Royalist cause. It reported:

The troopers, having missed their prey on the hills, (the gentlemen having withdrawne themselves), some of them came to the castle under a pretence to see it, but entrance being denyed them, the common soldiers used threatening language, casting out words implying some intentions to take the castle.

These threats were immediately denied by their commanders 'who better knew how to conceal their resolutions'.

When the rebels had dispersed, Mary pondered on what was her best course of action. A victory for King Charles and the Royalists was assured, she was in no

The front page of an issue of the Mercurius Rusticus.

doubt of that. It was simply a question of time. Meanwhile, her husband was away from home attending the king at Oxford, and he had taken most of the household staff with him, apart from five male servants and some female attendants. She was sure he would soon return but in the meantime her duty was clear. She could not possibly mount a suitable defence with the slender resources of manpower and womanpower at her disposal. She would therefore call upon some of the able-bodied men of the town to form a guard. After all, she had cannon, did she not, and the keys to one of the strongest castles in all the land?

The 'taking of this guard', according to *Mercurius Rusticus*:

> ...*as it secured her at home, so it rendered her suspect abroad ... whatsoever she sends out, or sends for in, is suspected; her ordinary provisions for her family are by some multiplied, and reported to be more than double what indeed they were, as if she had now an intention to victuall and man the castle against the forces of two Houses of Parliament.*

A few days later a messenger arrived with a letter from the Parliamentary Committee of Dorset demanding the surrender of the castle's four small pieces of ordnance. The reason given was that 'the islanders conceived strange jealousies that the peeces were mounted and put on their carriages'. The presumption was that they were set up in readiness to fire.

Mary decided to adopt a conciliatory approach. She despatched messengers to both Poole and Dorchester begging that the cannon might remain in the castle for her own defence. And to convince the islanders that they were not a threat, she offered to have them removed from their carriages. The committee responded by promising that she could keep the cannon in her possession – a promise upon which they would soon renege.

Chief Justice Sir John Bankes by Gilbert Jackson.
Photo: The National Trust

2
THE BANKES FAMILY AT CORFE

How did Lady Bankes come to find herself in this predicament? Born Mary Hawtrey, she came from a family of Norman descent who had arrived in England at the time of the Conquest and now lived at Ruislip in Middlesex. In 1618, when she was twenty, she married John Bankes, a twenty-nine-year-old London barrister, and was to bear him six sons and eight daughters.

John Bankes was born at Keswick in Cumberland, a town overshadowed by the great mountain of Skiddaw. His father, also John, was a rich merchant who in later life became a minister of religion.

At the grammar school in Keswick young John became proficient in Latin and mathematics and was admitted to Queen's College, Oxford, in 1604, at the age of fifteen, to read law but left without taking a degree. He then entered Gray's Inn in London, where he studied for seven years before being called to the Bar in 1614.

John Bankes must have inherited some of his father's business acumen for in 1622 a prudent investment in the graphite mines of Borrowdale in his native Cumberland provided him with a useful source of supplementary income. The 'lead' from these mines was of such pure quality that it was used in the manufacture of the finest pencils.

In the 1620s he became a Member of Parliament, first for

Dr John Bankes at the age of seventy-five, in the robes of a Doctor of Divinity, by Gilbert Jackson.
Photo: The National Trust

13

Wootton Bassett in Wiltshire and then for Morpeth in Lancashire. Thereafter his rise was rapid. In 1630 King Charles made him Attorney-General to his son Prince Charles, then a mere infant, and four years later he was appointed Attorney-General to the king and given a knighthood. In January 1640 Sir John was appointed Chief Justice of the Common Pleas, a division of the King's Court whose jurisdiction was confined to civil matters. Two years later the degree of Doctor of Laws was conferred upon him, and he was 'sworn of the Privy Council'.

Loyal as he was to his sovereign, he did not necessarily follow unquestioningly where his king led, which was not always to his advantage. Had he not, perhaps, opposed the Militia Bill, which placed all trained bands in the counties under Parliament's control, he may well have been offered the position of Lord Chancellor when it became vacant.

In 1635 John Bankes used the wealth he had accumulated to buy the one-time royal castle of Corfe on Dorset's Isle of Purbeck. It was, he considered, a property and estate commensurate with his high position – and with it came the additional titles of Lieutenant of the Isle of Purbeck and Constable of Corfe Castle.

Corfe had been a royal castle from the time of King William I until, in 1572, it was sold 'with its demesne lands, liberties and privileges' by Queen Elizabeth I to Sir Christopher Hatton for the sum of £4,761 18s 7d. Hatton, who was one of the Queen's favourite courtiers and later became Lord Chancellor, further strengthened the castle when England was threatened with invasion by the Spanish Armada.

When Hatton died unmarried in 1592 the castle passed to his nephew and heir, Sir William Hatton. He died childless in 1597, and his wife Lady Elizabeth made a second marriage – to Lord Chief Justice, Sir Edward Coke who died in 1634. It was from his widow that Sir John purchased Corfe Castle the following year.

The castle was antiquated, and to make it a fit place to live in cost its new owner a considerable amount of money. He had it finished to the height of seventeenth-century luxury – even the 'closed stool' kept in a closet next to the bedchamber had a velvet cover on its seat. And while the work of refurbishment was being done Lady Bankes, ever mindful of the comfort of her household servants, had the windows of the guardrooms of the two gatehouses glazed to protect the occupants from the winter cold. The Bankes's younger children were excited at the prospect of living in a genuine castle with arrow-slit windows and vast galleried halls. They might have expected that the stone walls of their new home would be hung with swords, shields and trophies of the chase. Instead they found them hung with woven or embroidered tapestries, some depicting classical scenes.

The rooms were full of furniture imported from France. There were cabinets of ebony with gilded fittings, chairs and couches upholstered in crimson velvet and satin cushions adorned the window-seats. Turkish and Persian carpets covered the floors, there were Indian quilts on the beds and in the master bedchamber there was a four-poster with the 'finest linen bedclothes and crimson drapes of silk'.

On the shelves in the great library was Sir John's magnificent collection of leather-bound books, embossed with gold leaf. On the walls were paintings by such fashionable artists of the day as Sir Anthony Vandyke and Sir Peter Lely, whose acquaintance Sir John had made when he was studying law at Gray's Inn. Occupying pride of place among them was a Vandyke portrait of Charles's queen, Henrietta Maria, which had been given to Sir John by his sovereign.

The remains of the great keep – the crowning glory of Corfe Castle.

3

CORFE AS A ROYAL CASTLE

The castle's crowning glory, its keep, was within the inner bailey, the surrounding walls of which had been built in the reign of William the Conqueror. They were 80ft high, 12ft thick, formed a 72ft by 60ft square and were constructed of local Purbeck stone. A south-facing annexe was added a little while later. The keep was all the more impressive because the summit of the hill upon which it stood was 150ft above the level of the ground below. It was originally a two-storeyed building with basement and attics, and was later altered to three storeys without any change being made to the exterior appearance. Of necessity, the roof was made of lead; all of the castle buildings had roofs either of this material or of tile or slate. Thatch, being highly combustible, could have been set alight by a single flaming arrow fired by an enemy.

The upper storeys were reached by a staircase which, like those of the two great gatehouses, wound upwards in a clockwise direction. This would oblige any right-handed aggressor who ventured to climb the stairs to use his sword in his left hand, whereas the defender could use his sword in his right.

The keep served not only as the castle's last line of defence, but until the reign of King John was the residence of the king when he visited the area. Its ground floor housed the kitchen and sleeping quarters of the cooks and servants. Here food was stored and a water supply was connected. For reasons of security, entry was always to the first floor, originally by wooden ladder or stairway, but latterly by a permanent stone staircase which led down to the rear of the inner gatehouse.

On the next floor was the great hall, its walls brightly painted and hung with rich and vivid tapestries. Here the king would hold magnificent feasts to the accompaniment of music played by minstrels in the gallery above. The hall also served as conference centre and courtroom for settling local disputes. The king, his family, his guests and personal servants slept on the top floor, where there was a private chapel for the exclusive use of the royal family and their most important guests.

It was King John who built the gloriette, meaning literally a highly decorated chamber, but in this case referring to all the buildings which he had newly

The keep or King's Tower, the gun terraces and inner gatehouse, and (below), the remains of the gloriette buildings at Corfe Castle.
Photo: The National Trust

constructed within the inner ward so that he would not have to suffer the discomforts of the cold and draughty keep. It consisted of new royal apartments, a chapel, a kitchen block, a bakery with two ovens, a wine cellar, two separate courtyards, a garden and a well.

John was unpopular with the people but was a capable king. In view of the reverses suffered by the English in France including the loss of Normandy, some of the £1,400 he spent on improving the castle went towards

King John's tomb effigy in Worcester Cathedral.

improving its defences. He died in 1216 at the age of forty-nine and was buried in Worcester Cathedral, where his tomb effigy is flanked by the smaller figures of two saints whom he admired, Oswald and Wulstan. He is the only English monarch to be buried in that cathedral and was the first one to have an effigy carved in Purbeck marble. John's son, Henry III, carried out more improvements at Corfe during his fifty-six-year reign.

Another £1,000 was spent on the structure, and a great deal of entertaining took place there. The exterior walls of the keep were whitewashed, and the interior walls plastered, painted and decorated with stencilled motifs, green being the colour in vogue. Rooms were adorned with lavish paintings, tapestries depicting hunting scenes, damask silks and armour. Some rooms were panelled.

The reign of King Edward (1272–1307) saw extensive restructuring of the buildings of the gloriette, to make the King's Hall, King's Presence Chamber, Long Chamber, King's Chapel and Queen's Chamber. Finally, in the first two years of the reign of King Richard II (1377–99), a new gloriette tower was added in the southeast corner of the inner ward. It had five chambers and cost £269 to build.

The last monarch to use the castle as a royal residence was Henry VII in 1496 and the Tudor

The Tudor royal coat of arms in a stained glass window.

Photo: Corfe Castle Town Trust

19

royal coat of arms in stained glass was placed in one of the windows. It was later removed by John Uvedale of More Crichel and placed in the window of a first-floor room in his house in East Street.

From 1212 until 1615 the Isle of Purbeck had been designated a Royal Hunting Reserve. Strangers were excluded and Purbeck provided sport for the king and his courtiers and meat for the tables of the royal palaces. No killing of deer was otherwise allowed and no inhabitant was permitted to build a wall, or bank or grow a hedge any higher than a deer could leap. All falcons nesting in Purbeck were the property of the king, as were all 'royal fish', namely porpoise, sturgeon and grampus – species hardly likely to be caught in its rivers or sea.

By the end of King Henry III's reign in 1272 the area had become largely disafforested and was given the less distinguished title of Warren of Coneys. However, the rights of hunting, even of rabbits, remained with the Crown. King James was the last monarch to exercise these rights in 1615.

From the keep's high watch-tower, vast areas of the Isle of Purbeck could be seen spread out in all directions in a landscape of rural tranquillity. To the west

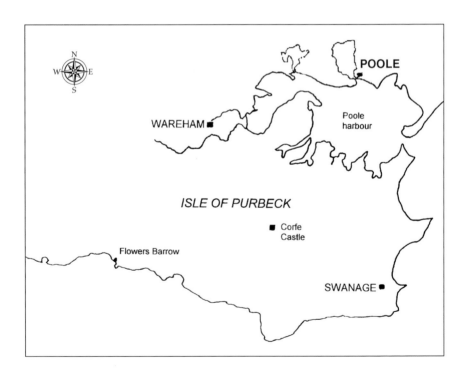

was Creech Barrow Hill, so-called because on its summit was an ancient burial ground. Here was situated a watch-tower, the occupant of which held the office and title of Keeper of the Deer. Beyond this, the westernmost boundary of Purbeck, was the Celtic coastal fort of Flowers Barrow on the cliff high above Worbarrow Bay, and a little stream called Luckford Lake which ran into the River Frome. To the south were lush green valleys and scattered farmsteads, the only settlement of any size being a little fishing village known as Sandwich (later to be called Swanage), and the waters of the English Channel.

To the east were the waters of Poole Bay and Studland Bay where white cliffs and pinnacle-shaped rocks, among them Old Harry and Old Harry's Wife, named after a famous pirate of former times and his spouse, jutted out from the sea at the end of the peninsula.

Purbeck's northern boundary, beyond a great expanse of heathland, was formed by Poole Harbour and the River Frome and its estuary. On this heath were to be found isolated dwellings inhabited by those who eked out a meagre existence as crofters. On the banks of the River Frome was Wareham, a town founded by the Saxons and fortified by King Alfred against the Danes.

4

THE CAUSES OF THE CIVIL WAR

The roots of the unfolding conflict dated back to the time of Charles's father James I. His ideas differed from those of his predecessors, Henry VIII and Elizabeth I, who often found it expedient to call on Parliament when they required support for their actions. James expected Parliament to be his useful servant and had little thought of consulting or of appraising himself of its wishes. Having dissolved his first two Parliaments, which he considered to be too much in favour of the Puritans, James reigned for seven years without finding it necessary to summon Parliament to meet at all.

When Charles's first Parliament met there was a widespread feeling that foreign affairs had been mismanaged by his father James, who had sent in 1619 an ill-equipped and ineffectual army to support the Protestant Elector Palatine of the Rhine and King of Bohemia, Frederick V, against the Roman Catholic Emperor of Bohemia. Then early in Charles's reign an equally ineffectual force, this time naval, was sent to attack Spain with equally predictable results. To prevent the impeachment of the Duke of Buckingham, who as Lord High Admiral was blamed for this failure, Charles dissolved Parliament. His popularity waned even further with his marriage to the Catholic princess Henrietta Maria, daughter of King Henry IV of France, and he was now forced to raise money directly from his subjects, and if they refused to pay he had them brought before the Court of Star Chamber which imposed heavy fines on them.

Charles's monetary demands became ever greater with the despatch in 1627 of an expedition, led by the Duke of Buckingham, to France to support the Huguenots against the Catholic King Louis XIII. Again the enterprise was a failure. Unrest at home brought about by economic hardship forced Charles to put the country under martial law. Soldiers were billeted in private houses and dissenters were tried and punished by army officers in military courts. However, a lack of income forced Charles to summon Parliament once again and this time he had to submit to its demands and grant the Petition of Right which became law in 1628. This ruled that no taxes or forced loans should be raised by the king without its consent, neither should anyone be imprisoned without a fair trial, nor should soldiers be billeted in the houses of private citizens, and citizens should not be tried in military courts.

When Parliament reassembled it was again in immediate dispute with the king. It offered to grant taxes on goods which passed through customs houses for one year but Charles wanted the grant for life. When Parliament proposed changes to church services, as advocated by the bishops, Charles dissolved it once again.

The Court of Star Chamber continued to exact monies from the king's subjects, and in addition Charles decided to revive an old tax known as ship-money, not only from seaports as had previously been the case but also from counties inland. This was to raise money for the navy, whose ships were falling into decay.

In religious matters, Charles relied on William Laud whom he made Archbishop of Canterbury. When Laud ordered that in every church in the land the altar should be placed at the east end and surrounded by a rail, and that on entering everyone should bow to the altar and the men remove their hats, the Puritans objected, seeing this as a return to the unnecessary ceremonial of pre-Reformation days.

Charles and Laud then proceeded to interfere in the affairs of the Presbyterian Church in Scotland. From henceforth, Presbyterian ministers in all churches would be required to use a prayer book specially drawn up by Archbishop Laud. This provoked a storm of indignation and in 1639 the Scots responded by raising an army which forced Charles to concede and grant them the right to worship in their own way. After this so-called 'Bishops' War' with Scotland, Thomas Wentworth, Charles's chief adviser on affairs of state whom he made Earl of Strafford, told the king that he would be stronger with Parliament's support than without it. Accordingly, the two Houses were recalled after a period of eleven years. However, the disagreements became so violent that Charles dissolved them within three weeks.

More problems with the Scottish Presbyterians left Charles in the invidious posi-tion of having to pay the invad-ing Scottish army to remain in England until an agreement could be reached. As the king

Archbishop Laud.

23

had no money in his coffers to do this he was
obliged to summon Parliament yet again.

In 1640 what was to become known
as the Long Parliament was led by John
Pym. Its first action was to call the
king's ministers to account for their
misrule, which had brought the
country to such a disastrous state.
Laud was impeached, as was Strafford,
who was beheaded for high treason.
The Court of Star Chamber was closed
and ship-money declared to be an
unlawful tax. The Triennial Act was
passed, by which Parliament was to meet at
least once every three years and could not be
dissolved without its own consent.

John Pym

Seeing his power ebbing away, Charles resolved on
one final desperate action to win it back. He would go in person to the House
of Commons and order the arrest of five of those members whom he considered
to be his worst enemies, one of whom was Pyme. The Commons, however, had
been forewarned and the attempt failed. The Speaker would not disclose the
whereabouts of the five, saying famously that he had 'neither eyes to see nor
tongue to speak', to which Charles responded bitterly, 'I see the birds have flown.'

The country polarised itself into two camps. Parliament demanded control of
the army and navy. Charles refused and left London to gather his Royalist forces
and prepare for war.

5

THE PROTAGONISTS PREPARE

Mary Bankes's response to the attack by the rebels on May Day was to start recruiting and arming a body of men at her own expense. She also managed to procure the services of a professional gunner.

Her sons John, Ralph, Edward, Jerome and Charles – potential heirs to the Bankes's estates – she decided to send at once to the safe-keeping of her daughter, Alice, and her son-in-law Sir John Borlase, who lived in Royalist Oxford.

In January 1642, the king had left London to travel north with the intention of raising an army. His first reverse of fortune came at Hull where the governor, Sir John Hotham, refused to surrender the town's reserves of arms, powder and shot which had been stockpiled for war with the Scots. After this humiliation Charles withdrew to York and there he set about rallying support for his cause.

John Bankes had initially remained at Westminster but was soon to be summoned by the king to join the Privy Council at York. He did not go empty-handed. Mary's account book, in which she detailed income and expediture, has survived and in it is the entry:

September 15 delivered to Mr Bankes at his going to York [£]*410. 00. 0.*

On 27 August 1642, the king raised his royal standard at Nottingham, an act which was effectively a formal declaration of war. The flag bore the king's arms – a hand pointing to a crown and the words 'Give Caesar his due.'

Alice Bankes, Lady Borlase, by Anthony Vandyke.
Photo: The National Trust

25

Nottingham

Ominously, the royal standard, as soon as it was raised, was blown down and could only be set up again with difficulty, owing to its great size and the force of the wind.

The Parliamentarians were also making their preparations. They drew their greatest support from London and the larger cities and towns. In Norfolk the Puritan leader, Oliver Cromwell, country gentleman and son of a Huntingdonshire squire and former Member for Cambridge of the Short and Long Parliaments, rallied all like-minded men to his cause.

Cromwell, who had studied at Cambridge with thoughts of becoming a barrister, played a principal part in the creation of the New Model Army with its emphasis on strict discipline and morality. Against his well-trained forces would be matched the cavalry of King Charles's dashing young nephew, Prince Rupert – the twenty-three-year-old son of Frederick of Bohemia and his wife Elizabeth, daughter of James VI and I of Scotland and England.

Two months later Charles marched south from Shrewsbury in Shropshire to attack London. This prompted the Parliamentary commander Robert Devereux, 3rd Earl of Essex, to move from Worcester to stop the king's advance. On 23 October 1642 the two armies, each numbering some 20,000 men, met at Edgehill in Warwickshire to fight the first major battle of the Civil War. Oliver Cromwell commanded a troop of horse.

At first Prince Rupert's cavalry had the initiative but, in their haste to pursue the enemy, they failed to notice that Essex had broken through the king's infantry and captured the royal standard. The battle was indecisive, neither side claiming victory. The standard was later recovered by one of the king's officers who managed to infiltrate the enemy's ranks by wearing an orange scarf captured from one of the Roundheads.

Oliver Cromwell.

Charles now entered Oxford and the city, the colleges of which had melted down their gold and silver plate to boost the royal coffers, now became the headquarters for himself and his court. In December 1643 he summoned a meeting of the Parliament, which consisted of those members, 118 in all, who had been driven from the House of Commons in London. It convened on 22 January 1644 in the Great Hall of Christchurch College. Among those present were Sir John Bankes and his son-in-law, Sir John Borlase, MP for Corfe Castle. As a result of the latter's attendance he was declared by the London House of Commons to have forfeited his seat at Corfe.

From Oxford, Charles marched once more towards London, but the strength of the forces ranged against him made him decide not to risk a confrontation. Mary could see that her husband was exhausted. She knew that he had not only given his monarch loyal service in his judicial capacity but had also been supplementing the royal finances with money from his Cumbrian graphite mines and his legal practice. She had noted in her account book on 8 March 1643:

...payd into the exc[h]equer for the king £166

Sir John had also brought money to the Crown by prosecuting, in 1637, a case in the Court of Star Chamber against one William Prynne who had studied law at

Sir John Borlase by Anthony Vandyke.
Photo: The National Trust

28

Lincoln's Inn, after which time he had busied himself by writing a number of controversial pamphlets. One, entitled *Histrio-Mastix, or a Scourge for Stage Players*, published in 1633, was said to contain matter defamatory to the king.

The ruling of the court was that Prynne be fined £5,000, have both his ears cut off, be pilloried as a public punishment and be imprisoned for life. Apparently undeterred by the physical discomfort awaiting him, Prynne made from prison a libellous attack on the Archbishop of Canterbury, William Laud, for which he was again fined, pilloried and this time branded on both cheeks with the letters 'S L' for Seditious Libeller. Prynne was later released and, against all the odds, became a Member of Parliament.

In the same year, 1637, Sir John represented the Crown in the case against John Hampden, a Member of Parliament who had played a prominent part in the drawing up of the Petition of Right. Hampden had also refused to pay the hated ship-money – which had been levied on all counties and not merely on coastal areas since 1635.

Lady Bankes, as the wife of the Lord Chief Justice, had met her sovereign several times on state occasions and at banquets, and had formed her own impression of his character. Charles was the second son of James I and Anne of Denmark and was born at Dunfermline Palace, 12 miles from Edinburgh, on 19 November 1600. He was a delicate child and even at the age of three he was still unable to walk or talk. He had never expected to be king and only became heir to the throne when his elder brother Henry – well-built, athletic and an expert in the joust – died unexpectedly in 1612 at the age of eighteen.

In contrast, Charles was short in stature and suffered from a stammer which he never managed to overcome. He came to the throne on 27 March 1625 on the death of his father, and within two months had married the diminutive sixteen-year-old Henrietta Maria, to whom he remained devoted until his death.

Charles was a home-loving person and a devoted father to his children. He ate little

King Charles I.

and seldom drank. He was not at all extravagant and was never more content than when playing real tennis or riding. He was a fine horseman and shared his late father's enthusiasm for hunting. He was a connoisseur of the arts and it was under his patronage that the Royal Collection of paintings and sculptures – of which there were more than 400 – became one of the most important in Europe.

At court, Charles insisted on formality. No one was allowed to sit in his presence, save for his wife and family. Between 1630 and 1644 the couple would have three sons, Charles, James and Henry, and three daughters Mary, Elizabeth and Henrietta.

As for the government of the country, Charles believed that he had a God-given right to rule his people – the so-called 'Divine Right of Kings'. 'I must avow that I owe the account of my actions to God alone', he said in 1628.

6
'THE LADY' CONFRONTS THE REBELS

When forty or so seamen arrived very early in the morning at the castle to demand all its pieces of ordnance, 'the Lady in person (early as it was), goes to the gates and desires to see their warrant', reported the *Mercurius Rusticus*. They produced one, signed by some of the Parliamentary commissioners, but instead of handing over the cannon Mary Bankes had them mounted on their carriages again by the only five men left in the castle, assisted, on her orders, by all the maid-servants. One of the guns was then loaded and fired. 'Which small thunder so affrighted the seamen that they all quitted the place and ran away,' continued the newspaper. 'They being gone, by beat of drumme, she summons helpe into the castle, and, upon the alarme given, a very considerable guard of tenants and friends came to her assistance.'

Word travelled further afield, and at least fifty muskets were brought into the castle by sympathisers from all over the Isle of Purbeck. This hastily assembled guard remained within the castle for about one week but the rebels had no inten-tion of allowing Mary any respite. Threatening letters arrived telling her what great forces would be sent to fetch the cannon if she would not 'by faire means be perswaded to deliver them…' The letters also threatened that if her helpers from the town opposed the handing over of the cannon their houses would be set on fire. Word of these threats got out and Mary found herself having to cope with weeping, wringing of hands, and 'clamorous oratory' of the wives, who arrived at the gates and tried to persuade their husbands to return home 'and not, by saving others, to expose their own houses to spoyle and ruine'.

The rebels then made a proclamation at Wareham that no beer, beef, or any other provisions were to be sold to Lady Bankes, and strict watches would be kept so that 'no messenger or intelligence shall passe into or out of the castle'. Having, as they thought, removed the means of provisioning the castle and believing it to be 'but slenderly furnished for a siege either with ammunition or with victuall', the rebels proposed a compromise. Lady Bankes was to deliver up 'those 4 small peeces, the biggest carrying not above a 3 pound bullet', and in their turn the rebels would permit her to 'enjoy the castle and armes in it in peace and quietnesse'.

Mary knew that she now had to rely on her mental wit and agility to overcome the enemy, rather than on any physical strength. The decision to surrender her cannon was not an easy one to make, but, as she predicted, the rebels now presumed the castle to be theirs, even though they had not actually captured it. Over-confidence now led the rebels to be 'remisse in their watches, negligent in their observations, not heeding what was brought in, nor taking care, as before, to intercept supplies...' Mary, on the other hand, made good use of their remiss behaviour and took the opportunity to furnish the castle with provisions of all sorts, including 'a hundrede and halfe of powder' – about 170lbs – and a quantity of ignitable cord for firing the guns.

When word came that the king's forces under the command of Prince Maurice, brother of Prince Rupert, and the Marquis of Hertford, Lieutenant General William Seymour, were advancing towards the town of Blandford, 18 miles to the north, she sent a messenger to them describing her present situation, pointing out the strategic importance of Corfe Castle and 'desiring their assistance'. Dorset, she pointed out, provided an essential link between the Royalist strongholds of Oxford and Exeter and were it to fall into the hands of the Parliamentarians their fleet might take advantage of its coastline as a place to land their soldiers.

The Marquis of Hertford responded by sending a troop of men, commanded by Captain Robert Lawrence, to reinforce the castle, the garrison of which now consisted of a total of eighty or so men, including some gentlemen and some tenants employed there by Lady Bankes. Another person of military experience among the castle's defenders was Captain Bond, an elderly soldier who was to share in the honour of the resistance.

Any potential attacker would have either to starve the garrison into submission, or to break down or scale the surrounding walls which were 25ft or more high and some 15ft thick. Shortage of water would not be a problem as the castle had two wells, one in the inner and one in the outer bailey. There would have to be rationing, not only of food for the household but also of fodder for the animals.

Crenellated stone walls had replaced the original wooden pallisades of Saxon times, when Corfe Castle was part of the great Manor of Kingston, held by the Abbey of St Mary and St Edward at Shaftesbury in the north of the county. Behind the crenellations was a parapet that ran around the entire perimeter, including the sides of the towers.

Any attempt to force the mighty outer gatehouse was, of course, doomed to failure, or for that matter, the inner gatehouse which had not one but two

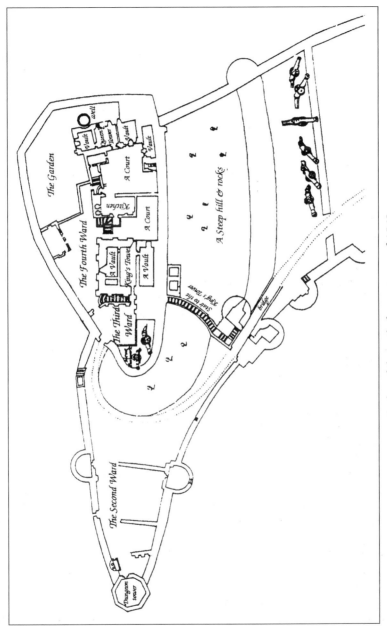

A plan of the castle from a survey of 1568.

The Garden

The Fourth Ward

The Third Ward

The Second Ward

Dungeon tower

Well

Vault

Queen's Tower

Vault

Vault

A Court

Kitchen

A Court

A Vault

King's Tower

A Vault

A Steep hill & rocks

Stair to the King's Tower

bridge

portcullises. Handily, above the guard-chamber of the inner gatehouse was an oubliette, a small room with neither doors nor windows, into which prisoners could be dropped through a trapdoor and forgotten.

Each bailey was a separately-defensible unit of towers linked by curtain walls and guarded by its own gatehouse. Each tower had a name – Cockayne, Plentey, Swalewe, Malemit, Sauveray, meaning 'Save the King' and Butavant, from the French 'to project forward'. The last three towers served as prisons.

The Plukenet Tower, built around 1270, was named after Alan de Plukenet who was Constable of the Castle around that time. High on the tower and carved in stone in high relief was his coat of arms, a shield supported by two hands. The motif on the shield was blazoned as 'five fusils in bend'.

An attacker who managed to gain entry to the outer bailey would then have to negotiate the great ditch, which ran across it. It had taken miners seven months to create this ditch in the spring of the year 1207, on the instructions of King John. Above it were two raised banks where Mary's cannon – now confiscated

The Plukenet arms on the tower.

by the rebels – had been sited. The bastion, a structure projecting from the south wall of the inner bailey, had also provided an excellent site for pieces of ordnance. Winter came, and then spring, and still Sir John did not return. Did Mary, alone at night in the four-poster with its 'finest linen bedclothes and crimson drapes of silk', dwell on all those dark deeds that had been done in this castle which she was determined to defend.

The most notorious was the killing in AD978 of the sixteen-year-old Edward I, whose father, King Edgar, had battled successfully against the Danes and could claim credit for the unification of most of England. When he died he left behind two sons, Edward, who had been born to his first wife, Aethelflaed, and Ethelred, the son of his second wife, the beautiful Elfrida, daughter of Ordgar, Earl of Devonshire.

The second version of Edward's assassination is depicted in this stained glass window in Wimborne Minster. It shows Elfrida offering her stepson some wine while an attacker prepares to strike.

There are two versions of what occured at Corfe on 15 March 978. The earliest said that Edward was on his way to visit his half-brother when he was stabbed to death by Ethelred's retainers, who were acting on their own initiative to further the interests of their young master. The version that appeared a century later, and includes some local topographical details, was that the murder had been planned, and perhaps even committed, by Queen Elfrida so that her son could ascend the throne. Edward, it said, had been hunting and was sitting on his horse just outside the castle gates, drinking from a goblet of wine which Elfrida, who was staying nearby, had just handed to him. Suddenly, either she, or one of her thegns, stabbed him. His horse bolted in fright, Edward fell off and was dragged along by the stirrup to the bottom of the hill where the Byle Brook ran down to an ancient corn mill called Boars Mill, by which time he was dead.

Elfrida had Edward's body concealed for a year in a disused well, then taken to Wareham to a little wooden church which stood by the River Frome where he was hastily buried. Two years later it was conveyed on a bier to the nunnery church at Shaftesbury where his tomb became a place of pilgrimage. Venerated as a martyr, in 1001 King Edward I was canonised and his bones declared to be sacred relics. Ethelred's reign was short and unsuccessful. He was badly advised and was never at the right place at the right time to repel the Danish invaders who eventually repossessed his kingdom. Hence his nickname – Ethelred the Unready.

It was at Corfe that William the Conqueror imprisoned his son Robert Curthose, Duke of Normandy. Robert had rebelled against his father and was captured following his defeat at the Battle of Tinchebrai in Normandy in 1106. Also imprisoned there by his father, King Richard I, was Griffin, Prince of Wales, who was constantly attempting to invade England from the principality in the twelfth century.

At night, when the wind was howling and the owls hooting, Mary may well have imagined that she could hear the groans of the twenty-four French knights King John had incarcerated in the castle's dungeons. The year was 1202, when Corfe served not only as a royal castle but also as a state prison. The knights were captured during the siege of the French castle of Mirabel, occupied by John's niece, Eleanora, and her brother Arthur, Duke of Brittany, who were claimants to the English throne. Eleanor was brought to England and imprisoned, along with a group of the French knights, in Corfe's dungeon towers. She was later transferred to Bristol, where she died. She was not maltreated during her imprisonment at Corfe. A tunic and supertunic of dark green was ordered for her, along with a dark brown cap with variegated fur known as miniver and a hood for inclement weather. She also had a saddle with gilded reins, which suggests that she was allowed a degree of freedom to ride out across the grassy downlands on her horse. When she fell ill a physician – Master John de Beauchamp – was summoned from London to attend her. For this he was paid the sum of three marks, about £2, but part of this was in compensation for the loss of his horse which had died on the return journey.

When the holy hermit Peter de Pomfret dared to predict the year in which the King John would lose his crown, he was bound to a horse's tail and dragged through the streets of Wareham and back to Corfe where he was hanged on a gibbet, along with his son. His prophesy proved to be correct, although he did not live to see it.

In 1327 Corfe was to play its part in the death of another English king. Edward II was deposed by his wife, Isabella, and held prisoner at Corfe before being taken to Berkeley Castle in Gloucestershire where he was nastily done to death.

So how would the present conflict be resolved? All Mary Bankes could do was to draw comfort from the fact that in all Corfe Castle's long history, it had never been taken by an enemy.

7
JUNE 1643: THE SECOND ATTACK

A volley of shots, of such intensity that it could only be from the enemy's cannon, rang out and sent everyone in the castle scurrying to their posts. A seemingly overwhelming force of between 200 and 300 cavalrymen and infantrymen was besieging the castle, and the gunfire was coming from the hills where they had sited two pieces of ordnance. Smoke was also rising from the town, the result of the rebels having set fire to four of its houses. Their anger had been aroused by Sir John Bankes's denunciation of the Earl of Essex, Lord Manchester and other Parliamentary leaders as guilty of high treason for continuing in arms against the king. Sir John was himself impeached in turn for high treason by the Roundhead Parliament in London, and he and his family were declared 'malignants' who must forfeit all their lands and property.

After the bombardment, the attackers once again summoned the castle to surrender, and once again they 'received a deniall' from Lady Bankes after which they withdrew.

A sixteenth-century saker – a long-muzzled cannon with a calibre of 90mm.
Photo: English Heritage

A helmet, cannon balls and breastplate and back plate of the Civil War period.
Photo: English Heritage

Gunners' tools (left to right): *A corkscrew-like 'worm' for removing traces of wadding after firing, a ladle for inserting the powder, a sponge for washing out the barrel, and a rammer for forcing down powder and shot.*
Photo: English Heritage

The period of eerie silence which followed was broken when, on 23 June 1643, Sir Walter Erle, Colonel of Horse and Foot and Lieutenant of the Ordnance, accompanied by three captains from the Poole garrison, namely William Sydenham, one of four brothers who had taken up arms for Parliament, Henry Jarvis and William Skut, with a body of between five and six hundred men, 'came and possessed themselves of the towne, taking the opportunity of a misty morning that they might find no resistance from the castle'.

Sir Walter Erle's father, Thomas Erle, was Member of Parliament for Wareham and a fierce critic of royal policy. Sir Walter had been knighted in 1616, in the thirteenth year of the reign of King James I, and it was during the previous year that he had raised a troop of horse consisting of fifty men, since when he had borne the rank of colonel. The family seat was Charborough, six miles north of Wareham.

The rebels' main encampment was in a field on the south side of Corfe town which became known as Battle Mead. Other troops were billeted in Corfe itself, and still more at nearby Church Knowle in terraced cottages on either side of the main street known as Higher Barracks and Lower Barracks.

This time the attackers were better prepared, bringing with them a demi-cannon, which threw a ball of between 30 and 36 lbs; a culverin which was smaller, but with a barrel of greater length which gave it greater accuracy; and two sakers. Cannon balls, some stone and others iron, hit the castle walls but bounced harm-lessly off, causing little or no damage. There was no necessity for the defenders to take any action at this stage, other than keep watch and make sure the gates were kept secure.

Suddenly, cannonfire came from another direction – from the motte and bailey known as The Rings. This was a large mound which provided a lookout point, beside which was a level area with accommodation, storerooms, stables, workshops, kitchen, a well and a chapel, the whole surrounded by a defensive earthen bank and ditch with timber palisade. The Rings, which lay to the west, had been constructed by King Stephen when he besieged the castle in 1139 during another period of civil strife. He was involved in an armed struggle with the Empress Matilda, daughter of Henry I and a claimant to the throne. On that occasion, however, the king found himself on the outside and attempting, by siege, to oust Baldwin de Redvers, 1st Earl of Devon, who was occupying it.

The Parliamentarians had chosen The Rings to site their cannon as from it they had a good field of fire. The disadvantage was that from here the distance to the castle was too great for the fire to be effective, and the defenders jeered as the shots fell short.

The rebel officers then, according to the *Mercuruis Rusticus,* resorted to more desperate measures and:

...to bind the souldiers by tye of conscience to an eager prosecution of the siege, they administer them an oath, and mutually binde themselves to most unchristian resolutions, that if they found the defendants obstinate not to yield, they would maintaine the siege to victory, and then deny quarter unto all, killing without mercy men, women and children.

Then they encouraged their men further by stating that of the forty men in the castle, twenty were willing to come over to the Parliamentarians' side, and that there was rich booty to be had from it:

All base and unworthy means were then used... to corrupt the defendants to betray the castle into their hand; the better sort they endeavour to corrupt with bribes, to the rest they offer double pay, and the whole plunder of the castle.

However, when all these efforts proved to be of no avail, they once more withdrew to think again and to build a siege engine which would enable them to get close enough to the castle walls and tunnel down and lay explosive charges.

The siege made Lady Bankes and her capable lieutenant, Captain Robert Lawrence, painfully aware of the great responsibility they bore in attempting to resist such vastly superior forces as the Parliamentarians were able to muster. They knew full well that they were putting at risk the lives of the household servants and the brave men of the town who were helping their cause. 'The Lady' was also aware how much the castle relied on the services of those on the outside – the grooms and huntsmen, carters and the farrier, tailors, cobblers, masons and many other craftsmen who skilled were no longer available to the besieged household.

A cover for surface mining was a planked roof on wheels. The roof and sides would be covered with skins to conceal and protect the occupants.

A hand-sewn shoe, found in 1962 during alterations to Hollands, now the National Trust gift shop at Corfe Castle.

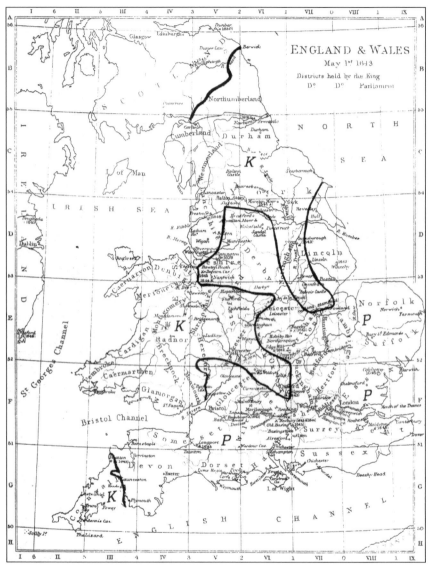

Districts favouring the opposing forces at 1 May 1643.
The K sectors are for the king, the P sectors for the Parliamentarians.

8

PREPARATIONS AT POOLE

It was from the town of Poole to the north that the assault on Corfe Castle, soon to enter a more brutal phase, was being orchestrated. Hitherto, Poole had been regarded only in its natural position as a flourishing maritime port; it was now to become a Parliamentary garrison town. Charles I and his ministers were particularly unpopular in Dorset. When the ship-money tax proved difficult to collect the Crown responded by seizing the cattle from those who refused to pay it and this caused great hardship, so much so that the county's Sheriff, John Freke, recorded bitterly that 'the tax was paid like drops of blood'.

When the Civil War began in August 1642, the county polarised itself into opposing camps. Wareham, Poole, Dorchester, Lyme Regis and Portland were for Parliament; Sherborne, Blandford, Corfe, Weymouth and Bridport for the king. Poole declared early against the king, and took prompt measures to organise effective assistance to the cause it had adopted. On 16 January 1642 a watch was set up to guard the town. It consisted of one watchman, one patrolman and one gunner for the daytime at the town gate, and six watchmen and two patrolmen for the night watch.

The Parliamentary Committee for Dorset held many of its meetings at Poole and took more steps to make the town secure on 1 July 1642:

An order was made by the Parliament for the defence of the town, authorising the mayor and aldermen to assemble the inhabitants of the town, or any others who might offer themselves as volunteers, and array and arm them for resisting any attacks that might be made upon the town, and to hinder the surprisal of the ordnance and magazine there.

The story is now taken up by schoolmaster and poet John Vicars (1580–1652), whose family, like that of Sir John Bankes, originated from Cumberland. Vicars was educated at Christ's Hospital and Queen's College, Oxford, and became a Puritan and a fierce opponent of Rome. His *England's Remembrancer* was the first and second part of a chronicle describing the fortunes of the Parliamentarians against the Cavaliers between 1641 and 1643. A third part followed in 1646. His account confirms that:

About the midst of August 1642 information came to the Parliament that the good townes of Dorchester and Poole, in Dorsetshire had bravely fortified themselves, and mounted their ordnance, and made strong defences to prevent the Marquis of Hertford's intention to have seized on them and their magazine, arms and ordnance.

Shortly afterwards the marquis sent a drummer to Poole requiring it to yield obedience to his commands for the king, promising to fortify that town most strongly for the greater security and safeguard of its inhabitants.

The mayor and the people of Poole, however, had other ideas. They answered that 'their towne was already very well fortified and provided with ordnance, horse and foot, to oppose any malignant whomsoever' and that the marquis 'if he did send any [forces] without their consent they would deny them entrance'.

By the first week of the following year, 1643, in addition to Poole, the towns of Dorchester, Lyme, Melcombe, Weymouth, Wareham and Portland were in the possession of Parliament. In February, Vicars records that the garrisons of Poole and Wareham defeated the Irish Royalist regiment of Murrough O'Brien, 1st Earl of Inchiquin – 'killed some, took several prisoners, two pieces of ordnance, and fired their magazine'. The Poole garrison also fell upon a convoy of Prince Rupert's, and captured 'money, £3,000, one hundred horse, arms and ammunition'.

Spurred on by its success the garrison, under the command of Sir Walter Erle, now felt sufficiently strong and confident to start the siege of Corfe Castle. Sir Walter is mockingly described in *Mercurius Rusticus* as:

...a sagacious knight ... that hath the gift of discerning treasons, and might have made up his nine and thirty treasons [to] forty, by reckoning in his own.

However, his letters reveal him to be an individual on the one hand desperately anxious to please his superiors, yet on the other without the wherewithal to fulfill their high expectations of him. His constant anxiety was that at any moment the Royalist army might attack him – which it did on several occasions. Wareham, which he made his headquarters, was to change hands several times during the war.

On 30 June 1643, when his bombardment of Corfe Castle from The Rings was failing to achieve its object, Sir Walter wrote to the Speaker of the House of Commons, William Lenthall. He informed him that since the departure of Prince

Maurice and Lord Hertford from Dorset and their overrunning of Devon and Somerset, his men's hearts 'have so failed them that they are not nearly so forward to engage their persons and estate as formerly they were'.

He goes on to complain about the difficulties of financing the campaign, saying that:

The levying of money, moreover, whereupon depends the maintenance of the local forces, is at a standstill; every man being afraid lest the bringing in of his money may expose him and his estate to plunder and rapine, should any strong party of the enemy break in upon the country – as is likely enough.

He adds that he is likely to be utterly ruined if he obeys all the commands which are laid upon him. For example, he has been ordered by the Parliamentary general, Sir William Waller, to march towards him with as many men as possible and at the same time is bidden by the Parliamentarians' Lord High Admiral, the Earl of Warwick, to provide nearly 300 musketeers for the fleet bound for the west. Neither of these demands, he asserts, are consistent with the safety of Dorset and those places of importance in it which until now have been safeguarded for Parliament. In fact, the demands are such that if either of them are obeyed, he, Walter Erle, will be brought into a far worse condition than ever he was in before. During the last twelve months, he had at least able to draw on two or three companies of foot, if necessary, beside his

Arms of Erle-Drax.
The motto translates as
'Death in a righteous cause'.

troop of horse. Now, however, when within 30 or 40 miles of him there are three bodies of enemy forces who may send out parties to attack Wareham he has only a single troop of horse to call upon. And all this at a time when he is upon the point of besieging, or at least blocking up, Corfe Castle, and when Portland, 20 miles to the east, 'begins to incline to a second revolt,' which will be effected more easily 'since Weymouth will be left without a garrison, as it will be if both these commands are obeyed'.

Portland Castle, a coastal artillery fort built by Henry VIII. It was designed to be part-circular in shape to make it stronger and more resistant to cannonfire.

Photo: English Heritage

On 11 July 1643 Sir Walter wrote again to the Speaker William Lenthall to voice his anxieties:

Honoured Sir ... Regarding the particular of Corfe Castle I have the Earle of Warwick's letters to shew ... that hee would with that assistance that I could afforde him undertake the worke, he giveing mee direction to hasten thitherward [to Corfe] as soone as I should heare of his putting forth from the Ile of Wight towards Studland Baye which I accordingly did upon the arrival of two of his shipps there: but afterwards understanding from his Lordshipp that haveing been kept back by contrary windes for the space of ten dayes, he had receaved order from the Committee of the Safety to hasten westwards toward the relief of Exeter...

Sir Walter's disappointment at this lack of seaborne reinforcement to materialise was somewhat ameliorated when the Earl of Warwick then sent word that he had:

...procured 2 great gunes from Portsmouth for mee, willing men with them to beginn the worke which I did as soone as the gunnes came by quartering somme of my men

46

in Corfe towne, the rest as they came in unto mee I placed on the other side of the
castle where the batteries were made.

However, Sir Walter decided to keep his troop of horse at Wareham where he would set up his headquarters and journey to and from Corfe every day, 'rather than to quit the place and runne such an hazzard as before I have mentioned...'
In conclusion the hapless Sir Walter wrote:

So as you may see in what an unhappy condicion I am to be censured for my actions
... only I desire and make it my humble request that the House would bee pleased
(at least as part of a recompense for the faithful service that I have done them), to give
mee the hearing in the makeing of this my apologie and vindicating myselfe from
those aspersions which have been unjustly cast upon mee.

Had she known about this correspondence it might have amused Mary Bankes to know what inconvenience, not to say embarrassment, she was causing to members of the Parliamentary hierarchy who, with greatly superior forces, were having such difficulty in dislodging her and her small band of defenders from their stronghold.

9

AUGUST 1643: NO SURRENDER

A t first light an astonishing sight met the eyes of the watchers in the castle. A
large caterpillar-like vehicle had laboriously crossed the ditch and was
approaching the walls up the grassy bank. As it drew nearer they could see that
its roof and sides were covered in sheepskins; it travelled on three wheels; and it
was propelled by men on the inside, only the legs of whom were visible.

Following behind this siege engine, which the defenders nicknamed the
Sow, was an even larger one, which they called the Boar. The attackers' intention
was obvious. They were planning to place the siege engines up against the
castle walls, and, under their protective cover, attempt to tunnel down and plant
explosives.

The defenders waited until the first siege engine was within pointblank range
and then opened fire. There was a deafening cacophony of sound, and when the
smoke cleared it was evident that the Sow was not musket-proof and had 'cast
nine of eleven of her farrow'. The marksmen from the castle had aimed at the legs
of the attackers, 'the onely part of all their bodies left without defence', with the
result that nine ran away, 'as well as their broken and battered legs would give them
leave, and of the two which knew neither how to run away … one was slaine'.
Whereupon the Boar, 'seeing the ill sucesse of the Sowe … cast her litter before
her time' and 'durst not advance'.

Mercurious Rusticus carries on in much the same vein, paying particular atten-
tion to the activities of Sir Walter, which apparently caused those inside the castle
walls no small degree of amusement:

> …*it was a general observation that valiant Sir Walter never willingly exposed himself
> to any hazard, for being by chance endangered by a bullet shot through his coat, after-
> wards he put on a beares skinne, and to the eternal honour of this knight's valour, be
> it recorded, for feare of musquet-shot he was seen to creep on all foure on the sides of
> the hill, to keep himselfe out of danger. This base cowardisme in the assaylants added
> courage and resolution to the defendants; therefore, not compell'd by want, but rather
> to brave the rebels, they sallyed out and brought in eight cows and a bull into the*

castle, without the losse of a man, or a man wounded. At another time five boyes fetcht in foure cows.

The meat and milk from these animals would make a welcome addition to the castle's stock of food, should the siege go on for any length of time. But the Parliamentarians, 'having spent much time and ammunition, and some men' in their attempt to undermine the walls, were 'still as farre from hopes of taking the castle as the first day they came thither'.

The commanders decided on another change of tactics – they would go up and over, not down and under the wall surrounding the castle. The Earl of Warwick sent them 150 mariners from Poole:

...the hope being that those experienced in shinning up the rigging of ships and climbing out along their spars might be successful in scaling the castle walls.

With them came:

Severall cart-loads of petards, grenades, and other warlike provision, with scaling ladders to assault the castle by.

The first man to scale the wall was offered the sum of £20 and so on, by descending amounts, to the twentieth who would receive £1. But these were not troops fighting for a cause or their country. They were mostly men taken out of gaol – 'silly wretches who were brought hither, as themselves confessed, like sheep to the slaughter'. When the commanders found that they could not bribe the men they had been sent from Poole, they decided to make them drunk, hoping that they would fight like lions.

'To this purpose they fill them with strong waters, even to madnesse, and ready they are now for any designe...' said the *Mercurius Rusticus,* adding that Sir Walter was 'the onely man almost that came sober to the assault'.

Two parties bore down upon the castle with scaling ladders. One attacked the west bailey, which was defended by Captain Lawrence who had with him the greater part of the castle's defensive force. The other party attacked the inner ward which Lady Bankes, with her daughters, women, and five soldiers occupied. The women were more than a match for the mariners. Lady Bankes 'did bravely performe what she undertooke', her little party heaving over stones and hot embers from the battlements in order to prevent the attackers from scaling their ladders and hurling the flaming torches they were carrying into the castle.

Replica of a half-suit of body armour of the Civil War period.
Photo: English Heritage

The Parliamentarians were once again repelled – 'having in this siege and this assault lost and hurt an hundred men.' The defenders lost only two men.

Sir Walter Erle 'cryed, and ran away crying', leaving Captain Sydenham to bring back the ordnance, ammunition, and the remainder of the army; 'who, afraid to appeare abroad, kept sanctuary in the church till night, meaning to suppe and run away by starrelight...'

When news came that the king's forces were approaching, Sydenham also fled, leaving his artillery, ammunition, and a good supper on the table:

Replica of a padded vest worn beneath the breast and back plates of body armour.
Photo: English Heritage

...and ran away to take boat for Poole; leaving likewise at the shore about an hundred horse, to the next takers, which next day proved good prize to the souldiers of the castle.

When Walter Erle learned that the Royalists, led by the Earl of Caernarvon, had taken Dorchester he moved his headquarters from Wareham to Southampton, explaining, in a letter dated 3 August 1653 to the Speaker of the House of Commons that:

I stayed without making my retreat as long as I could, so long that the news coming to Wareham of the taking of Dorchester, those few Foot which were in my quarter forsook their guards and got away leaving me in a malignant town with only 40 horse attending me.

Once again, Captain Sydenham was ordered to supervise the retreat and bring the ammunition, which he was forced to abandon when he realised that the Royalists were almost upon him.

Another Royalist newspaper, *Mercurius Aulicus*, gives details of a spiteful incident which occurred after the siege. Smarting after his defeat, even though his armoury had included siege engines and two huge 36-pounder guns whereas the defenders had no ordnance whatsoever, Sir Walter Erle out of revenge sent a party to the house of Sir Edward Lawrence, father of Captain Lawrence, the governor of Corfe Castle and commander of its garrison. Sir Edward's wife was forced to flee into the woods to save her life and the house, Creech Grange, which lay 3 miles east of Corfe at the foot of the Purbeck Hills, was plundered to such a degree that only the walls were left standing. The paper gave the number of rebels killed in their final assault on the castle as sixty.

Dorset's county treasurer kept accounts of the amounts paid by the Parliamentarians for their various requirements. These included £2 3s 4d, (£2.16p) for boards, hair, and wool for the Sow siege engine; 6s 0d (30p) for three truckle wheels for the Sow; and £266 12s 3d (£266.61p) for 'powder, match and bullets for the gunners'. Also listed was £1 12s (£1.60p) for 'a firkin of hot waters for the soldiers when they scaled the castle'. It omits to say for what purpose the firkin of hot water was used, but it may have been to add to the liquor, possibly rum or brandy, that the soldiers were given by way of Dutch courage.

10

QUIET DAYS AT CORFE

In the autumn of 1643 Mary's prayers were answered and her husband returned to Corfe Castle. He had been prevented from doing so earlier because of the overwhelming presence of Parliamentary forces in the vicinity of Wareham and the patrols mounted by the Earl of Warwick's vessels along the coast.

Sir John was told all about the dramatic events of the siege and introduced, for the first time, to little Arabella who had been born in the previous year. For his part he brought news of their sons, who were still with their married sister Alice Borlase in Oxfordshire. The eldest, John, who was now seventeen, had just gone up to Oriel College, Oxford, as a freshman for the Michaelmas term.

As for the progress of the war – Sir John could see little chance of a speedy resolution of the differences between the king and Parliament. His visit was, of necessity, short. He had to return to his duties as a judge at Salisbury Assizes, from which he had taken temporary leave of absence, and afterwards he would be required to attend the king again.

The Bankes family took the opportunity to enjoy a brief period of tranquillity, the Parliamentarians having for the time being at least, decided to leave them alone. They also took the opportunity to replenish the castle's stocks of food and munitions, for who was to know when their opponents might try again?

They rode out every day, not only to give encouragement to their loyal supporters in the town but also to keep abreast of the latest news. With their older daughters on their favourite ponies, they would ride up Brescombe Hill and up again along Nine Barrow Down where each ancient tumulus was said to mark the place where a great chieftain of old was buried. At the top they had a choice. They could take the winding path down into Studland, a hamlet renowned for being the centre of piracy in the reign of Queen Elizabeth I. From Studland's foreshore on a clear day the Isle of Wight was clearly visible, and little could they have known that soon King Charles would face the ignomony of being imprisoned there, in Carisbrook Castle. They might take the path along the top of Ballard Down and on to the end of the peninsula where white stack-rocks jutted out into a sea which on one day might race around the headland turbulently and

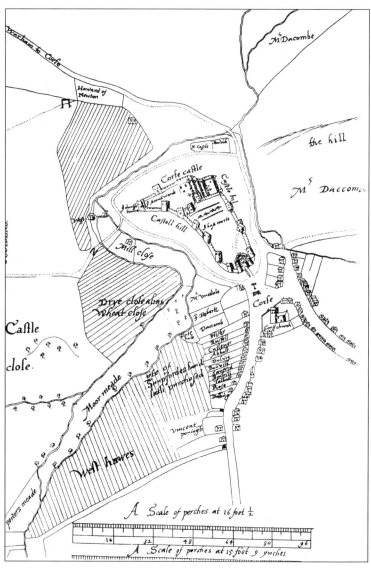

Map of Corfe and the surrounding countryside in the seventeenth century.

on another day lie flat and undisturbed. The third possibility was to turn south to Swanage, then a little fishing village so cut off from civilisation that the inhabitants bartered instead of using coin currency, and looked upon strangers as foreigners.

Another favourite ride was through Corfe's market square, with its forbidding wooden stocks which were a constant warning to potential miscreants, and its stone cross which was a focus for ceremonial occasions and celebrations. On the south side of the square was an elegant bow-fronted building which served as the mayor's robing room. By virtue of his office the mayor of Corfe was also a magistrate. Beyond the rectory

The fifteenth-century seal of the mayor and barons of Corfe.
Photo: Corfe Castle Town Trust

and the town hall the street was lined with cottages, many of which were owned by the castle and paid rent. The Bankes family also charged for the digging of clay on land which they owned in Purbeck. This was used in the manufacture of clay pipes. Further up the hill were the Halves, medieval field-strips used by the townspeople to grow their crops, the boundaries of each being marked by stones bearing the initials of the owner.

At the top of the street was the common, its landscape still bearing the scars made by horse-drawn sledges used to haul the stone and marble, mined from the quarries of Afflington and Blashenwell, into the marbler's yards to be dressed. The records of the Company of Marblers and Stone-Cutters of the Isle of Purbeck were destroyed by fire in the seventeenth century so the date of its formation is not known. However, it is believed to date from the reign of King Henry III (1216–72) and was probably the first guild of craftsmen ever to have been formed in England.

The Bankes family had one last duty to perform – a visit to the thirteenth-century Church of St Edward, King and Martyr, which lay just across the street from the castle's outer gatehouse. Although the castle had a chapel of its own, the family had sometimes attended the town's church – Mary for a ceremony known as churching, at which a mother gives thanks for the safe delivery of her child. On these occasions it was customary to pay the doctor who had attended the birth a fee, usually of 20 shillings.

The 65ft-high tower, was a fifteenth-century addition, and if the inhabitants of the castle were ever in any doubt as to what time of day it was, they need have no fear because a clock in the tower chimed the hour.

The church was unusual in that in 1578 it became a Royal Peculiar, and its rectors were appointed directly by the Crown, rather than by the diocese. The town also had its own Royal Peculiar Court which assembled periodically in the castle to try matters relating to church law.

Carved in stone above the tower's doorway were effigies believed to be those of John of Gaunt's eldest son, John Beaufort, and of his wife, Margaret. Beaufort was made Constable of Corfe Castle in 1397, the post having originated in 1203. Other heads on the outside of the tower arch are believed to represent John Beaufort's grandparents, King Edward III and his queen, Philippa, and John of Gaunt's third wife, Katherine Swynford. The presence of these effigies has led to speculation that the Beaufort family may have provided funds for the erection of the tower, which was built around 1400.

The mace of the Constables of Corfe is made of silver on an iron core and almost certainly dates from the late-fourteenth century when the Beauforts first held this office. It is 22 inches long and the tail – originally its head – is engraved with the Beaufort badge. The gadrooned head was added in 1692 and bears the royal arms of King William III.

When the Bankes family visited the church in the company of its rector, the Reverend Nicholas Gibbon, they were horrified at the scenes of despoilation that met their eyes. The churchyard had been used by the rebels as a battery for their siege guns, and tombstones were lying scattered and broken everywhere. Lead had been cut from the church roof and rolled into balls to serve as bullets for their muskets, and the doors of the church had been ripped off to provide cover for the troops assaulting the castle.

Inside, scattered about on the floor, were the remains of prayer books and parish registers which had been wantonly destroyed. A medieval reredos, made of Purbeck marble, had been smashed to pieces. The church organ was in tatters, its pipes torn down and used to serve as cases to hold powder and shot. The lid of the font lay on the floor and, judging by its murky contents, had been used as a drinking trough for the horses which, from the presence of straw on the floor, seemed to have been stabled within the church.

Sir John's departure for Salisbury to resume his judicial duties brought to an end the brief respite of normality enjoyed by the family, for whom the last few months had been a tremendous ordeal. It was at Christmas that Lady Mary realised she was pregnant once again but she resolved that, in spite of her condition, she would continue to resist the enemy at her gates. She asked her maid to attend to her hair, donned her finest satin gown

The font was fortunately not damaged when it did duty as a horse trough.

embroidered in gold and silver thread, with delicate lace at the cuffs, and put on the string of pearls that her loving husband had given her. Now she was ready to face whatever the fates had in store.

What she did not expect was the news that her husband had died on 28 December in Oxford at the home of his son-in-law, Sir Robert Jenkinson. His two eldest daughters, Sir Robert's wife Mary and her sister Alice, had been with him at the end. He had continued in his duties as Privy Councillor right up until the day of his death at the age of fifty-five.

Mary and her daughters made the journey from Corfe to Oxford for the funeral, a lavish and expensive affair befitting a person of such high status. In her account book, under the heading for 'The charge of the sickness and funerall of Sir John Bankes December 1644', is listed:

for funerall carriages of things when I came away	*£1 8s 0d*
for 2 horses a bridle and saddle for the journey	*£1 13s 0d*
for the hire of a coach for the journey making 3 days	*£3 0s 0d*

to the 3 doctors that attended my lord in his sickness	£22 0s 0d
the apothecarie's bill £15 16s 9d and	£3 07s 0d
paid to the Heralds, and for church clerkes at Christchurch	£27 11s 0d
for coffin, further Heralds men	£3 06s 0d
mournings for my sonne sonne in law brother & the gentlemen	£78 0s 0d
for black bages [drapes] to hand the roome & keep for my chamber	£16 0s 0d
mournings for my 4 daughters	£25 12s 0d
the tailor's bill for making them	£10 9s 0d

In addition there was a bill of £22 for making mournings for Mary's mother and her three sisters as well as 'expenses to the college' of £4 3s 8d for 'cooks, butlers, groomes,' making the total cost of the funeral nearly £240.

Sir John was buried in Christchurch Cathedral, and a monument was erected there to his memory.

11

WAR COMES TO WAREHAM

If the Parliamentary forces were ever to capture Corfe Castle, it was essential for them to gain firm control of Wareham, the gateway to Purbeck, which was once again in Royalist hands. To this end, on 23 November 1643, Parliamentary forces from Poole raided Wareham by sailing from Poole Harbour up the River Frome, and on the following day sent a more powerful force in the shape of the Parliamentary fleet under the command of Lord High Admiral, the Earl of Warwick. Five small vessels belonging to the Royalists were captured and by the end of the year the town was occupied by a garrison of troops under the command of Captain Francis Sydenham, younger brother of William.

On 21 January 1644 the Royalists struck back. Sir Ralph Hopton captured Wareham and took 300 prisoners, allegedly through the treachery of a Captain Morton, Captain of the Watch on the night of the attack, who was killed in the ensuing struggle. Lieutenant Colonel Henry O'Brien, brother of Lord Inchquin, was then installed as governor, and most of Dorset was now in the hands of the king.

The success of the Royalists in the West Country now alarmed the Derby House Committee which, under Parliament, controlled the army. In March 1644 a letter was sent to Sir William Waller, urging him to join forces with Sir William Balfour at Petersfield in Hampshire and strike back. By June, however, the fortunes of Parliament were again in the ascendant, the king having been dislodged from the Thames Valley and retreated to Worcester. The way was now open for an offensive in the west, and the Parliamentary commander, the Earl of Essex, accordingly swept into Dorset. On 16 June Weymouth surrendered, quickly followed by Dorchester. Essex demanded that Wareham surrender but O'Brien refused, his forces having been significantly increased with the arrival of 500 or so men from Lyme who had been withdrawn when the Royalists abandoned the siege of that town.

An alliance, made in September 1643 between Parliament and the Scots, and known as the Solemn League and Covenant, paved the way in July 1644 for an Anglo-Scottish army to crush the army of Charles I at Marston Moor just outside the city of York.

On 3 August 1644 the Derby House Committee, exasperated by the lack of progress, entrusted the capture of Wareham to Sir Anthony Ashley Cooper, and gave him the title Field Marshal General. Sir Anthony, a former Royalist who had changed his allegiance to the Parliamentary side, together with Captain William Sydenham laid siege to Wareham with 1,200 men. Soon afterwards they were joined by Lieutenant-General John Middleton with 1,000 horsemen. O'Brien, depressed by news from Ireland that his brother Lord Inchiquin had made terms with Parliament, having quarrelled with Charles I over the future of the Protestant Church, decided to surrender. The terms for the surrender were approved by the House of Commons on 14 August. The way was now open for the Parliamentarians to attack Corfe Castle once again, but it was to be another eighteen months before this was to happen.

The spring of 1645 passed without major incident, the rebels consolidating their tenure of Wareham by drawing in troops of horse and foot from the garrisons of Poole, Lulworth and Weymouth. Lady Bankes may or may not have been aware that Corfe Castle was, by the end of April, the only place in Dorset still to hold out for the king, with the sole exception of Portland. By October, Corfe would be the only royal garrison remaining between Exeter in Devonshire and London.

Not everyone in Corfe was sympathetic to the Royalist cause. Richard Brine, a tradesman of the town, complained that he had been utterly undone by the castle garrison, who had taken away his goods to the value of £200, pulled down two of his houses there, and carried the stones from the ruined houses into the castle 'to annoy the besiegers'.

However, on 20 June, the castle in turn was to suffer a considerable material loss. Colonel Robert Butler, the governor of Wareham, heard that the garrison at Corfe were in the habit of turning out their cattle and horses to graze by day and bringing them back into the castle by night. Accordingly, with Captains Jordan and Laurence and a party of horse and foot, he went there by night and lay undiscovered until daybreak when the garrison duly turned out the animals.

Colonel Butler approached the castle with his regiment of horse and faced them. His two captains, meanwhile, drew up the foot and entered the town of Corfe, and while Colonel Butler's cavalry was driving the animals away, the infantry prevented those of the garrison who had emerged from the castle from re-entering. At least 140 cattle and 20 good horses were seized in this way by the Parliamentarians, and all of them were brought safely to Wareham without a man being lost. The loss of the cattle and the horses was to cause much hardship to the occupants of the castle during the winter months.

In early February of the following year, 1646, Mary Bankes was astonished to find a party of 120 Cavaliers at the castle gates, under the command of a Colonel

The Earl of Essex, commander of the
Parliamentary army from July 1642.

James Cromwell – a distant relative of Oliver Cromwell, who had chosen to fight on the opposing side. She was even more astonished to see that they were holding as their prisoner Colonel Butler, the governor of Wareham.

Passing through Wareham on their way to Corfe, the Cavaliers had told the Roundhead sentinels that they belonged to Fairfax's regiment. Thomas, 3rd Baron Fairfax, was a Yorkshireman and a professional soldier who, with Oliver Cromwell, had been instrumental in creating the New Model Army. He had succeeded the Earl of Essex as commander-in-chief of the Parliamentary forces and his greatest triumph to date was the Battle of Naseby, fought on 14 June 1645.

As Colonel Cromwell's men wore scarves of similar colour to those of Fairfax's soldiers, their story was believed and they were permitted to enter the town. Colonel Butler, however, recognised them as the enemy and managed in the nick of time to bar the doorway of his headquarters to them. For three hours he and his son held out, until the Royalists set fire to a house next to the gunpowder magazine. At this point Colonel Butler wisely decided to surrender.

The Cavaliers took him with them to Corfe, where they found that the castle was encircled by a besieging force of superior size. However, the Parliamentarians, rather than jeopardise the safety of Wareham's governor, permitted them to pass through the picket lines.

Colonel Butler later managed to escape from Corfe Castle and, to the dismay of its defenders, persuaded Captain Lawrence who had defended it so valiantly, to defect and to accompany him in his flight. The pair could hardly have passed through the outer gatehouse without being apprehended, and it is more likely that they escaped through a sally-port – a doorway, usually on the first floor of the outside of a tower, through which a person could pass and be lowered down secretly at night to spy on the enemy.

James Cromwell's effrontery alarmed the Derby House Committee and on 12 February it ordered the Parliamentary cavalry, commanded by Colonel John Fitz-James, to remain in Dorset and six days later urged the Governor of Chichester to send 100 infantrymen to Corfe to relieve men who would otherwise have been guarding Wareham. For the occupants of Corfe Castle, the noose was beginning to tighten.

12

BETRAYAL

Colonel Henry Anketil, Corfe Castle's new governor, was also a Doctor of Divinity and was known to the the Roundheads as 'Colonel Ancketill the Priest and Malignant Doctour'. Late in February 1646 he was approached by a Lieutenant-Colonel Pitman, an officer of the castle's garrison who had served under the Earl of Inchiquin in Ireland. Pitman offered to fetch 100 men out of Somersetshire to reinforce the garrison and to seek leave of Colonel Bingham, the rebels' commander, for the colonel's brother who was a prisoner of the Parliamentarians, to be exchanged for one of the rebel officers who was held prisoner in the castle.

The first Mary Bankes knew of anything being amiss was when she was woken from sleep during the night of 26 February by a tremendous commotion. Pitman had arrived at the outer gateway with reinforcements as agreed. They included 100 men of the Weymouth garrison who had marched to Lulworth Castle where they had been joined by about forty more.

When about half the contingent had entered the castle Colonel Anketil said he could not accommodate any more and ordered the gates to be shut. Pitman expostulated with him, saying he had brought the men so far, at hazard to their lives, and now they were to be exposed to the cold and the enemy. The governor stood firm, still unaware that Pitman had changed sides and had duped him into admitting some seventy Roundhead soldiers.

Once inside the castle walls the Parliamentarians attacked under cover of darkness and quickly secured the King's Keep and Queen's Towers, and the two gun emplacements of the outer bailey. When daylight came, those troops who had been denied entry to the castle, took up station outside. Now, on seeing their friends on the towers and platforms, they advanced on the gates. Here they met no resistance, for the besieged, finding they were betrayed, demanded a parley.

No sooner had the truce been agreed upon than two of the rebels scaled the wall by ladder and were fired upon by the garrison. However, further confrontation was avoided and it was agreed that the lives of all the defenders should be spared, and 'those who were of the town should return quietly to their houses'.

The keys of Corfe Castle, the largest of which is 7 inches long.

These cannon balls, joined by a chain, were found in the moat.
They were often fired in pairs in naval warfare to inflict the
maximum damage to masts and rigging.

64

In all, 140 prisoners were taken, including Lady Bankes and her family. Only two of the garrison were slain and the attackers lost but one man in the action. Inside the castle the victors discovered a 'store of victuals and plunder, seventeen barrels of powder with match etc.' and thirty Parliamentary prisoners who were released.

At last, for Mary and her followers, the long ordeal was over. The following month, April 1646, the only other place in Dorset which still held out for the king, namely Portland, finally succumbed to Parliamentary pressure. As the surrender was a negotiated one, the members of Portland's Royalist garrison were allowed the honours of war, and marched out with their weapons, colours displayed, and drums beating.

When Corfe Castle fell it was systematically looted and numerous artefacts were dispersed among other manor houses in Dorset. Sir Walter Erle was responsible for the removal of all manner of contents, which was perhaps understandable in view of the fact that his own family home of Charborough had been burnt down by the Royalists.

Mary lost everything, including even her personal effects such as a satin petticoat in crimson, stomacher and sleeves lined with six silver laces, a bed with feather mattress, her favourite red chair upholstered in velvet and even her sweet bag and pomander. Paintings, furniture, tapestries, rugs – all were gone, including Sir John's library which, in October 1645, was granted to Sir John Maynard, Cromwell's sergeant. In any event the Bankes family would not have been permitted to retain their possessions because the Act of Indemnity and Oblivion, passed by Parliament in 1643, obliged Parliamentary leaders to confiscate the property of all those who had opposed them. However, as a mark of her courage, Mary was permitted to retain the keys and seals of the castle and a spur and cannon balls from the siege.

She and her children moved to London, perhaps to join her mother at the family home at Ruislip. Her father had died eight years previously.

True to form, Mary appealed against the order sequestrating her property and the Dorset Committee of Sequestration wrote to London concerning the 'difficulties arising before us concerning the Lady Bankes'. The committee replied stating that since her husband's death:

...she hath peticioned us to enjoy her jointure settled on her before the Delinquency of her husband ... wee, fynding her active in the defence of Corfe Castle against the Parlyament during her coverture, have not granted her desire.

However, on 27 February 1647 the sequestration order was lifted and, after the payment of a considerable sum of money, Mary and her children were able to

Armorial binding by Jean de Planche on one of two books from the library that have survived.

Photo: The National Trust

66

regain their family property. For this she 'compounded for herself at the sum of £455' and 'for her children at £370'. John, her eldest son, 'compounded at £1,974'.

Following the lifting of the sequestration order, her son, Ralph, made determined efforts to 'trace out the present possessors of the plunder of Corfe Castle'. However, all he managed to recover were two books, one large bed minus the feathers, one red velvet chair and a number of oil paintings of his family.

In March 1646 a vote was passed in the House of Commons for the demolition of Corfe Castle by mining and explosives, and a Captain Hughes, governor of Lulworth Castle, was appointed to undertake the work. The walls and towers were thrown down or blown up, and so great was the force of the explosion beneath the inner gateway that it rent the building in two. Stone and timber from the castle was appropriated by some of the gentlemen of the county, who had supported the cause of Parliament, for their own use. Most of the lead from the roofs was sold to a plumber of Poole.

On 14 June 1645, eight months before the fall of Corfe Castle, the battle that decided the Civil War had taken place just outside the Northamptonshire town of Naseby. There the 15,000-strong New Model Army, led by Cromwell and Fairfax, faced a Royalist army half its size and was victorious. In the process the king's cabinet, which contained his correspondence, was captured and it yielded up to the Parliamentarians many of his secret plans. Charles fled into Wales for safety, there to muster fresh forces.

Early in 1646 Fairfax approached Oxford, where the king had taken refuge. Charles slipped out of the city by night in disguise, and gave himself up to the Scottish Covenanters, who were currently besieging the town of Newark. From this vantage point he began to negotiate yet again with Parliament, which demanded complete control of the army and navy for twenty years, the abolition of the government of the Church by the bishops and the establishment of a Presbyterian Church. The Scots urged the king to accept these terms but he refused to commit himself so they handed him over to Parliament and on receiving back pay totalling £400,000, returned to Scotland.

Charles was now a prisoner of the Parliamentary army, which lodged him comfortably at Hampton Court Palace. From there he he escaped to Carisbrooke Castle on the Isle of Wight, believing that its governor, Colonel Hammond, would prove to be a friend. He was wrong, and was kept there under restraint. While attempting to negotiate with Parliament for his release he was simultaneously engaged in duplicitous negotiations with the Scots for their army to invade England, which it did, only to be routed in a few hours by Cromwell's Ironsides at Preston in 1648.

During that year there were revolts in Kent, East Anglia, South Wales, and the West and North Ridings of Yorkshire, areas which had previously seen little fighting. Primarily instrumental in stirring up passions was John Lilburne, leader of a movement known as the Levellers, who argued that with the imprisonment of the king, one tyranny had been replaced by another. The Levellers, who believed that all citizens had a right to participate fully in a democratic state and that everybody should be permitted to believe and practise whatever form of Christianity they wished, aimed to 'level out' the differences between the rich and the poor. Some called the revolts a second Civil War though this is perhaps an overstatement.

Early in 1649 Parliament decided the king should be tried for waging war against his own kingdom and against the Parliament, which had been purged by Colonel Pride and his regiment of foot in December 1648 of those still willing to negotiate with Charles. The Presbyterian majority was ejected and the fifty-three Independents who remained to form the Rump Parliament created a High Court of Justices to try the king for treason. Presided over by John Bradshaw, it had 135 members, among them Oliver Cromwell and his son-in-law Henry Ireton, but less than half that number attended every session of the trial that began on 20 January at Westminster Hall.

On 27 January, after thirty-two witnesses had been examined, a guilty verdict was returned. The sixty-eight members of the court present that day had agreed that when the king was sentenced that afternoon, 'to be put to death by the severing of his head from his body' they would all stand up simultaneously as a token of their unanimous agreement with the verdict.

The sentence was carried out on the morning of 30 January in front of the Banqueting House in Whitehall. Ironically, it was Charles's father James I who, in 1619, had commissioned the architect Inigo Jones to design a banqueting hall to replace the one which had been destroyed by fire. In one of its ceiling panels by Dutch artist, Peter Paul Rubens, King James was depicted as the bringer of peace and tranquillity.

Attended by his chaplain, Bishop Juxon, Charles walked to the scaffold from St James's Palace where he had been confined. It was a cold day and he wore two shirts in case he should shiver and the public mistake this for fear.

'I go from a corruptible Crown to an incorruptible Crown,' said the king to the bishop, 'where no disturbance can be, no disturbance in the world.' His final word to his chaplain was: 'Remember.'

His body was buried secretly at Windsor Castle. There was no state funeral and public mourning was banned. After his death his wife Queen Henrietta Maria returned to France, where she stayed until her own death in 1669.

England was now a republic, and a Council of State was appointed with the intensely religious Oliver Cromwell as its chairman. At first this council ruled through the Rump Parliament, whose fifty-three members had supported the call for the trial of the late king.

In May 1649 there was a mutiny in the army. Cromwell moved swiftly against the instigators and three of them were shot. He then proceeded to Oxford to receive an honorary degree from the city whose colleges six years earlier had been strong in their support for the king.

Success in England was followed by success in Ireland. With Cromwell in command of an army of 15,000 men the power of rebellious Irish Catholic Royalists was broken in nine short months. At Drogheda in August 1649, almost the entire population of some 3,000 was put to the sword, including priests and the garrison which had surrendered and been disarmed. This massacre was, it was said, retribution for atrocities committed by the Irish against English and Scottish Protestant settlers in 1641.

In 1650 the Scottish Royalists were defeated at Dunbar. In the summer of the following year the Scots, having once again invaded England, were defeated by Cromwell at Worcester. On this occasion they were led by the late king's twenty-year-old son, Charles, who had been crowned king at Scone on 1 January. Charles, who was hidden by Royalist sympathisers, survived as a fugitive for six weeks with a price of £1,000 on his head, after which he fled into exile, first to France and later to Holland.

The Rump Parliament consisted largely of avaricious moneylenders and lawyers, and it reminded Cromwell of the Parliaments of Charles I, which he considered to be ungodly. Not only that but it obstructed his reforms so, in April 1653, he abolished it using the same heavy-handed tactics for which he had criticised the late king. 'You have sat too long here for any good you have been doing,' he raged. 'Depart, I say, and let us have done with you. In the name of God, go!'

He then created in place of Parliament an assembly of 140 men who were nominated by the army and the Independent Congregational churches. This arrangement however also proved to be unworkable and collapsed within a few months. At this point Cromwell, having been offered it, could have accepted the throne himself. Instead he chose to govern as Lord Protector and Head of State with a council of fifteen. In September 1654 the first Protectorate Parliament came into being, with 400 Members for England and Wales and 30 each for Scotland and Ireland. Under the Protectorate, Jews were permitted to worship openly for the first time in more than 300 years.

Cromwell's years as Lord Protector were marked by further outstanding military achievements. At sea, the Dutch were defeated by the brilliant English Admiral, Robert Blake, and Jamaica was captured from the Spanish. However, at home Cromwell found it increasingly difficult to govern. Although life in the counties began to recover from the trauma and devastation of the war, the many country gentlemen who were elected to the new Parliament again reminded Cromwell of the privilege and corruption of the past and he saw this as the return of Royalism via the back door.

In 1655 Cromwell dismissed the first Protectorate Parliament and proceeded to divide England and Wales into eleven districts, each ruled by a major-general whom he hoped would bring righteousness to the shires. Within two years this experiment had also failed and the rule of the major-generals was abolished by the second Protectorate Parliament.

Oliver Cromwell may be described as a pious and unsmiling man who was ruthless and merciless on God's behalf. Although as both politician and soldier he had a unique insight into the problems of his country, under his rule the concept of Merrie England ceased to exist. Music and the theatre were regarded as frivolous, lust was a sin, fornicators were imprisoned, and the celebration of Christmas was forbidden. Lawyers who questioned the validity of his edicts were imprisoned and clergymen who preached what he regarded as heresy were defrocked.

On 3 September 1658 Oliver Cromwell died at the age of fifty-nine and was replaced as Lord Protector by his son, Richard. In 1659 the Rump Parliament was recalled, but now a power struggle developed and it was dismissed by the army.

Eighteen months after Oliver Cromwell's death, a section of the army under General Monck decided that it was time for free elections to be held and for the monarchy to be restored.

13
THE RESTORATION

In 1660 Charles returned from Holland, and entered London on 29 May – his thirtieth birthday. John Evelyn recorded in his diary:

> This day came His Majesty to London, after a sad and long exile, with a triumph of twenty thousand horse and foot, brandishing their swords and shouting with inexpressible joy, the way strewn with flowers, the bells ringing. I stood in the Strand and beheld it and blessed God, and all this without one single loss of blood, and by that very army which had rebelled against him.

Charles was crowned on 23 April the following year by William Juxon, Archbishop of Canterbury, who had attended his late father on the scaffold twelve years previously.

Charles II's reign was to be colourful, his libertarian ideas being in sharp contrast to the stifling Puritanism of Oliver Cromwell. However, like his father before him, he was not above intrigue, and he set about negotiating secret treaties with Louis XIV of France, appointed Roman Catholics to his government, and did not disapprove when his brother James, Duke of York, openly converted to Catholicism. In 1662 he married Catherine of Braganza, daughter of the King of Portugal, but this did not deter him from having a succession of mistresses, including the Duchess of Portsmouth. However, his favourite was the actress Nell Gwynne, whom he met in 1668 at the theatre.

Two disasters were to strike the City of London during Charles's reign. An outbreak of bubonic plague in 1665 killed one person in six, and the Great Fire in 1666 destroyed more than 13,000 homes and many famous buildings, including St Paul's Cathedral. This gave Christopher Wren the opportunity to design a new St Paul's. His designs, however, displeased the king and the Church's Protestant hierarchy, and had to be changed. One criticism was that the proposed new building lacked a nave and there would, therefore, be nowhere for the choir to sit.

Following the Restoration there was a court case and Sir Walter Erle was

Charborough House.

ordered to return to the Bankes family all the property which he had looted from Corfe Castle. The only item not to be returned was a wooden beam which had been used as a floor-joist when Charborough House, which had been destroyed by the Royalists in the Civil War, was rebuilt during the period of the Commonwealth. Sir Walter was allowed to keep this beam on payment of 'a valuable consideration'.

14

MARY BANKES: THE LAST YEARS

Lady Mary Bankes's life of sixty-three years spanned the reigns of a queen, three kings and the Commonwealth. In that time the country changed from being a monarchy, with Parliament doing little more than rubber-stamping the instructions of the sovereign, into a Parliamentary democracy, albeit an embryonic one. Both monarch and Parliament had, in the meantime, looked down the barrel of a gun, or in this case a musket, and realised that neither could comfortably co-exist without the other.

Mary Bankes's heroic stand at Corfe Castle was recognised by both friend and foe alike. Her life, and that of her family and friends were spared, and she was eventually permitted to regain her estates, albeit at a price, and live unmolested for the remainder of her days secure in the knowledge that she had done her duty as she saw it. She spent her final years at Damory Court, Blandford, Dorset, and had the immense satisfaction of seeing King Charles II enthroned, and her son, Ralph, knighted at Canterbury for the 'loyal services of his house' to the late king.

She died suddenly on 11 April 1661. She had been in good health to the last and, wrote George Bankes in his *History of Corfe Castle* published in 1853:

She gave to her relatives so little expectation of her death, that her eldest son, then absent from her, being in Dorsetshire, was married on the morning of the day she died.

On the south wall of the chancel of St Martin's Church, Ruislip, where many of Mary's Hawtrey ancestors are buried, is a memorial tablet to her erected by her son. It bears the inscription:

TO THE MEMORY OF THE LADY MARY BANKES, YE ONLY DAUGHTER OF
RALPH HAWTREY, OF RUISLIPP, IN THE COUNTY OF MIDDX., ESQUIRE
THE WIFE AND WIDOW OF THE HONBLE SR JOHN BANKES, KNIGHT, LATE
LORD CHIEFE JUSTICE OF HIS MAJESTYES COURT OF COMMON PLEAS,
AND OF THE PRIVY COUNCELL TO HIS LATE MAJESTY KING CHARLES THE
FIRST OF BLESSED MEMORY WHO HAVING HAD THE HONOUR TO HAVE

BORNE WITH A CONSTANCY AND COURAGE ABOVE HER SEX, A NOBLE
PROPORCION OF THE LATE CALAMITIES, AND THE HAPPINESS TO HAVE
OUTLIVED THEM SO FARR AS TO HAVE SEENE THE RESTITUTION OF THE
GOVERNMENT, WITH GREAT PEACE OF MIND LAID DOWN HER MOST
DESIRED LIFE THE 11TH DAY OF APRIL 1661.
SIR RALPH BANKES HER SON AND HEIR HATH DEDICATED THIS.

Mary Bankes's old adversary, Sir Walter Erle, died in the autumn of 1665 at the age of sixty-seven and was buried at Charborough Park.

Of the Bankes's thirteen children, seven died young or unmarried. Their eldest son, John, travelled in 1646 to France and Italy. He did not marry, and died in 1656 at the age of thirty. Their second son, Ralph, probably accompanied his brother on his Grand Tour of Europe before going up to Oxford in 1648. He represented Corfe Castle in Richard Cromwell's Parliament in 1653 and in 1660 he was re-elected by the same constituency to the first Parliament of Charles II's reign. The following year he married Mary Brune of Athelhampton in Dorset, and the couple had a son and heir, John, who was born in 1665.

Jerome, the youngest surviving son, also studied at Oxford and in 1654 visited Rome. He died unmarried in 1686. All the Bankes sons were, like their father, avid book collectors.

Youngest daughter Arabella Bankes by Peter Lely, and her brother Jerome Bankes by Massimo Stanzione. Photos: The National Trust

74

The armorial bearings of three generations of the Bankes family in a window of St Stephen's Church, Kingston Lacy. The glass was originally in a window of Wimborne Minster.

Alice, the eldest daughter who had married Sir John Borlase, converted to Roman Catholicism when she was widowed in 1672 and died eleven years later in Paris where she had devoted her days to good works and caring for the poor. Mary, the second daughter, married Sir Robert Jenkinson, 1st Baronet of Walcot and Hawkesbury in 1653. She died in 1691. Joan, the third daughter, married William Borlase, and Jane, the fifth daughter, whose date of death is unknown, did not marry. Arabella, the sixth daughter, married Samuel Gilly of High Hall, Wimborne. The date of her death is also unknown.

Ralph inherited the family estates which included, as well as Corfe, the manor of Kingston Lacy which lies to the northwest of Wimborne. It is believed to have been the site of a former palace of the West Saxon kings, and it was of sufficient importance as an administrative centre to have five royal visits in the reign of King Edward I alone. James I gave the manor to Sir Charles Blount, 1st Earl of Devonshire, who had played an important role in the pacification of Ireland. From him it passed to his son, Mountjoy Blount, who sold it in 1636 to Ralph's father, Sir John Bankes, for the sum of £11,400.

Immediately after the Restoration, Ralph, who remained a Member of Parliament until his death in 1677, started building a new house at Kingston Lacy, which he was to call Kingston Hall. His architect was Roger Pratt. Above the chimneypiece in the library, he hung the iron keys and red seals of Corfe Castle, which the Parliamentary commander Colonel Bingham had allowed his mother to retain after the siege.

Kingston Hall.
Photo: The National Trust

CONSTABLES OF CORFE CASTLE 1205–1504

1205 William de Blundevil
1205 Galfrid de Nevil
1207 John de Bassingbun
1215, 20, 30 Peter de Mauley
Anno incento★ Luke de Cary
1221 John Russel
1224 Joscelyn de Wells, Bishop of Bath
1224 Randulph Gernum
1238 Richard de Langeford
1241 Hugh de Vivon
1248 Peter Genevil
1249, 53 Bartholomew Peche
1250, 51, 52, 55, 72, 75, 76 Elias de Rabayne
1258 Stephen Longspe
1260 Matthew de Mara
1260 Philip Basset
1262 Nicholas de Moels
1263 Peter de Montforte
1264 Henry of Almaine
1269 Roger Mortimer (2)
1269 Alan de Plukenet
1280 Richard de Bosco
1281 John de Cormailes
1299 William de Montacute
1299 Simon de Montacute
1301 Henry de Laci, Earl of Lincoln
1305 Robert Fitz-pain

1306 William de Montacute, 2nd baron
1330 William de Montacute, 3rd baron
1314 Philip Walwayne
1315 Richard Lovel
1320 John Rycher
1320 Roger Damory
1322 John de Latimer
1325 John Peche
1330 John Matravers
1339 Thomas Cary Knt.
Anno incento★ Sir John Deverell
1341 Ralph de Ufford
1344 Philip de Weston
1346 Sir John Grey of Ruthyn
1359 Roger Mortimer, 2nd Earl of March and Ulster
1363, 68, 76 John de Elmerugg
1372 John de Arundel
1390 Thomas Holland, 2nd Earl of Kent
1392 John Bach
1397–1461 Beauforts, Earls and Dukes of Somerset
1462 Richard Plantagenet, 3rd Duke of Gloucester
1485 Sir John Turberville
1504 Henry Uvedale of More Crichel

★ year unrecorded

BIBLIOGRAPHY

Bankes, George. *The Story of Corfe Castle.* John Murray, London, 1853

Bankes, Viola and Walkin, Pamela. *A Kingston Lacy Childhood.* The Dovecote Press, 1986. *A Dorset Heritage: The Story of Kingston Lacy.* Anthony Mott, London 1953

Bayley, A R. *The Great Civil War in Dorset.* Barnicott & Pearce, The Wessex Press, 1910

Bond, Thomas. *The History and Description of Corfe Castle.* Edward Stanford, London, 1883

Broughton, Harry. *Wareham.* Printed by Anglebury-Bartlett, Wareham and Swanage, Cameron, K, edit. *The Place Names of Dorset.* English Place-Names Society, 1977

Fraser, Antonia, edit. *The Lives of the Kings and Queens of England.* Weidenfield & Nicholson, London

Fry, Plantagenet Somerset. *Kings and Queens.* Dorling Kindersley, London, 1990

Gardiner, S R. *Atlas of English History.* Longmans, Green & Co., London, 1907

Hill, C P. *Who's Who in History.* Basil Blackwell, Oxford, 1965

Hutchins, John. *The History and Antiquities of the County of Dorset,* 1774

Jones, Barry and Dixon, M V. *The Macmillan Dictionary of National Biography.* Papermac 1982

Masefield, Muriel. *The House of History.* Thomas Nelson & Sons, 1931

Robinson, C E. *Picturesque Rambles in the Isle of Purbeck,* 1882

Royal Commission on Historical Monuments (England). *An Inventory of Historical Monuments in the County of Dorset,* HMSO

Sibun, Doris. *Dorset Brasses and the Persons They Commemorate.* The Abbey Press, Sherbourne, 1974

Tinniswood, Adrian and McDonald, Andrew. *Corfe Castle 1,000 Years of History.* The National Trust

Trenchard, Diana. *Women of Dorset.* Dorset Books, 1994

Treves, Sir Frederick. *Highways and Byways in Dorset.* Macmillan, 1906

GUIDES

Corfe Castle. The National Trust, 1999

The Church of St Edward, King and Martyr, a Guide and History. William Pitfield & Company, Dorchester

The Church of St Edward, King and Martyr. The National Trust

Kingston Lacy. The National Trust, 1994

Portland Castle. English Heritage

INDEX